JOHN RUTTER

ELEGY AND FESTIVE BELLS

MUSIC DEPARTMENT

OXFORD
UNIVERSITY PRESS

for Ian McMillan

1. Elegy

JOHN RUTTER

*mellow solo stop

© Collegium Music Publications 2019. Exclusively licensed worldwide to Oxford University Press.

Printed in Great Britain

OXFORD UNIVERSITY PRESS MUSIC DEPARTMENT, GREAT CLARENDON STREET, OXFORD OX2 6DP

The Moral Rights of the Composer have been asserted. Photocopying this copyright material is ILLEGAL.

25
a tempo
Gt.
31
pochiss. rit.
a tempo
35
Celeste
40
Gt.
(Gt.)
poco a poco cresc.

poco stringendo
allargando
45
(cresc. sempre)
Maestoso
49
rit.
f
Sw. mf
mp
Tranquillo, come prima
55
p
Gt.
62
Sw.
mp

68
poco rit.
74
a tempo
p
Gt.
82
rit.
a tempo, poco più tranquillo
rall.
89
rall. al fine
Sw.
mp
molto legato
p
pp
3

2. Festive Bells

JOHN RUTTER

19
24
cresc.
f
29
Sw.
34
mf

37
Sw.
Gt. or Ch.
41
45
49

53
Gt.
p cresc. poco a poco
Sw.
mf cresc.
Gt.
57
non legato
f
allargando
Largamente e trionfale ♩ = c. 120
62
ff
67
mf

72
cresc.
f cresc.
77
molto rall.
Allegro, come prima
ff
81
+ Tpt.
85
senza rit.
fff